AWESOME DOGS

Bernese Mountain Dogs

by Rebecca Sabelko

BLASTOFF! READERS
2

BELLWETHER MEDIA • MINNEAPOLIS, MN

Note to Librarians, Teachers, and Parents:

Blastoff! Readers are carefully developed by literacy experts and combine standards-based content with developmentally appropriate text.

Level 1 provides the most support through repetition of high-frequency words, light text, predictable sentence patterns, and strong visual support.

Level 2 offers early readers a bit more challenge through varied simple sentences, increased text load, and less repetition of high-frequency words.

Level 3 advances early-fluent readers toward fluency through increased text and concept load, less reliance on visuals, longer sentences, and more literary language.

Level 4 builds reading stamina by providing more text per page, increased use of punctuation, greater variation in sentence patterns, and increasingly challenging vocabulary.

Level 5 encourages children to move from "learning to read" to "reading to learn" by providing even more text, varied writing styles, and less familiar topics.

Whichever book is right for your reader, Blastoff! Readers are the perfect books to build confidence and encourage a love of reading that will last a lifetime!

This edition first published in 2018 by Bellwether Media, Inc.

No part of this publication may be reproduced in whole or in part without written permission of the publisher. For information regarding permission, write to Bellwether Media, Inc., Attention: Permissions Department, 5357 Penn Avenue South, Minneapolis, MN 55419.

Library of Congress Cataloging-in-Publication Data

Names: Sabelko, Rebecca, author.
Title: Bernese Mountain Dogs / by Rebecca Sabelko.
Other titles: Blastoff! Readers. 2, Awesome Dogs.
Description: Minneapolis, MN : Bellwether Media, Inc., [2018] | Series: Blastoff! Readers: Awesome Dogs | Audience: Ages 5-8. | Audience: K to Grade 3. | Includes bibliographical references and index.
Identifiers: LCCN 2017028765 | ISBN 9781626177390 (hardcover : alk. paper) | ISBN 9781681034546 (ebook)
Subjects: LCSH: Bernese mountain dog--Juvenile literature. | Dog breeds--Juvenile literature.
Classification: LCC SF429.B47 S23 2018 | DDC 636.73--dc23
LC record available at https://lccn.loc.gov/2017028765

Editor: Betsy Rathburn   Designer: Tamara JM Peterson

Printed in the United States of America, North Mankato, MN.

Table of **Contents**

Bernese mountain dogs are a huge dog **breed**. They are calm and lovable pets.

4

These furry friends are often called Berners.

Bernese Mountain Dog Profile

wide, flat head

triangle-shaped ears

double coat

Life Span: 7 to 10 years

Trainability:

(1) (2) (3) (4) (5) (6)

Hardest to train   Easiest to train

Berners are gentle giants.
They can weigh up to
120 pounds (54 kilograms)!

These dogs have powerful
legs and deep chests.

Berners have large heads with friendly eyes. They often look like they are smiling.

They have floppy, triangle-shaped
ears and long, bushy tails.

Berners have heavy double **coats**. Their **tri-color** fur is long and soft.

Bernese Mountain Dog Coats

rust

tan

Most Berners are black with white and **rust** markings. They can also be black, white, and tan.

History of Bernese Mountain Dogs

Berners lived in the mountains of Switzerland for **centuries**.

Switzerland

N
W — E
S

There, they became **loyal** farm dogs. They guarded farmyards and pulled milk carts.

In 1926, a man named Isaac Schiess brought Berners to the United States. He owned two on his Kansas farm.

Berners joined the **Working Group** of the **American Kennel Club** in 1937.

Berners are cheerful **companions**. They like to learn and play.

Their favorite activities
are spending time outside
and practicing tricks.

Some Berners are
competitive. They show
off their skills in dog sports.

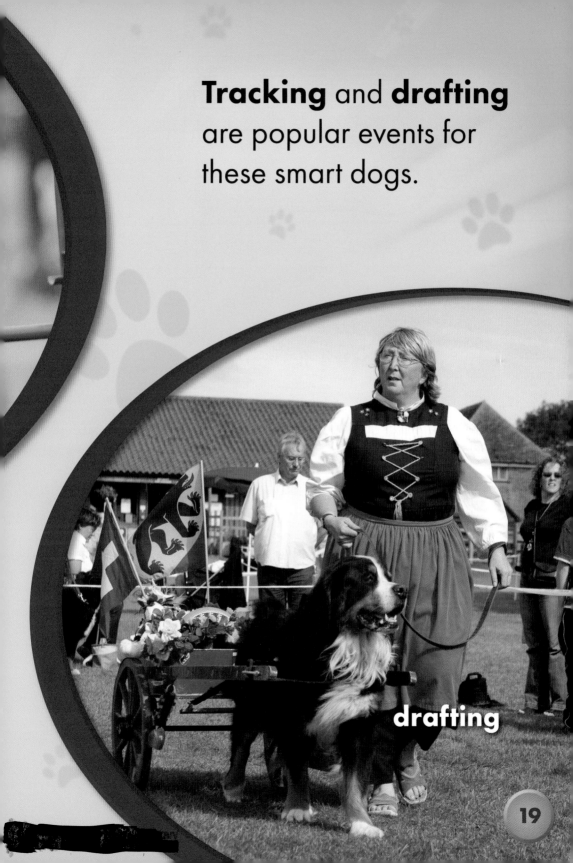

Tracking and **drafting** are popular events for these smart dogs.

drafting

19

Berners need lots of attention. They want to be included in every family event.

These dogs love their
human friends!

Glossary

American Kennel Club—an organization that keeps track of dog breeds in the United States

breed—a type of dog

centuries—hundreds of years

coats—the hair or fur covering some animals

companions—friends who keep someone company

competitive—trying hard to win or succeed

drafting—pulling a cart filled with goods

loyal—having constant support for someone

rust—a reddish brown color

tracking—following a scent

tri-color—a pattern that has three colors

Working Group—a group of dog breeds that have a history of performing jobs for people

To Learn More

AT THE LIBRARY

Bozzo, Linda. *I Like Bernese Mountain Dogs!*
New York, N.Y.: Enslow Publishing, 2017.

Morey, Allan. *Bernese Mountain Dogs.* North
Mankato, Minn.: Capstone Press, 2016.

Sommer, Nathan. *Saint Bernards.* Minneapolis,
Minn.: Bellwether Media, 2018.

ON THE WEB
Learning more about
Bernese mountain dogs
is as easy as 1, 2, 3.

1. Go to www.factsurfer.com.

2. Enter "Bernese mountain dogs"
   into the search box.

3. Click the "Surf" button and you will
   see a list of related web sites.

With factsurfer.com, finding more information
is just a click away.

Index